Contents

1 Families

- Read words
- Use new words

Student Book page 5

Aiden's family

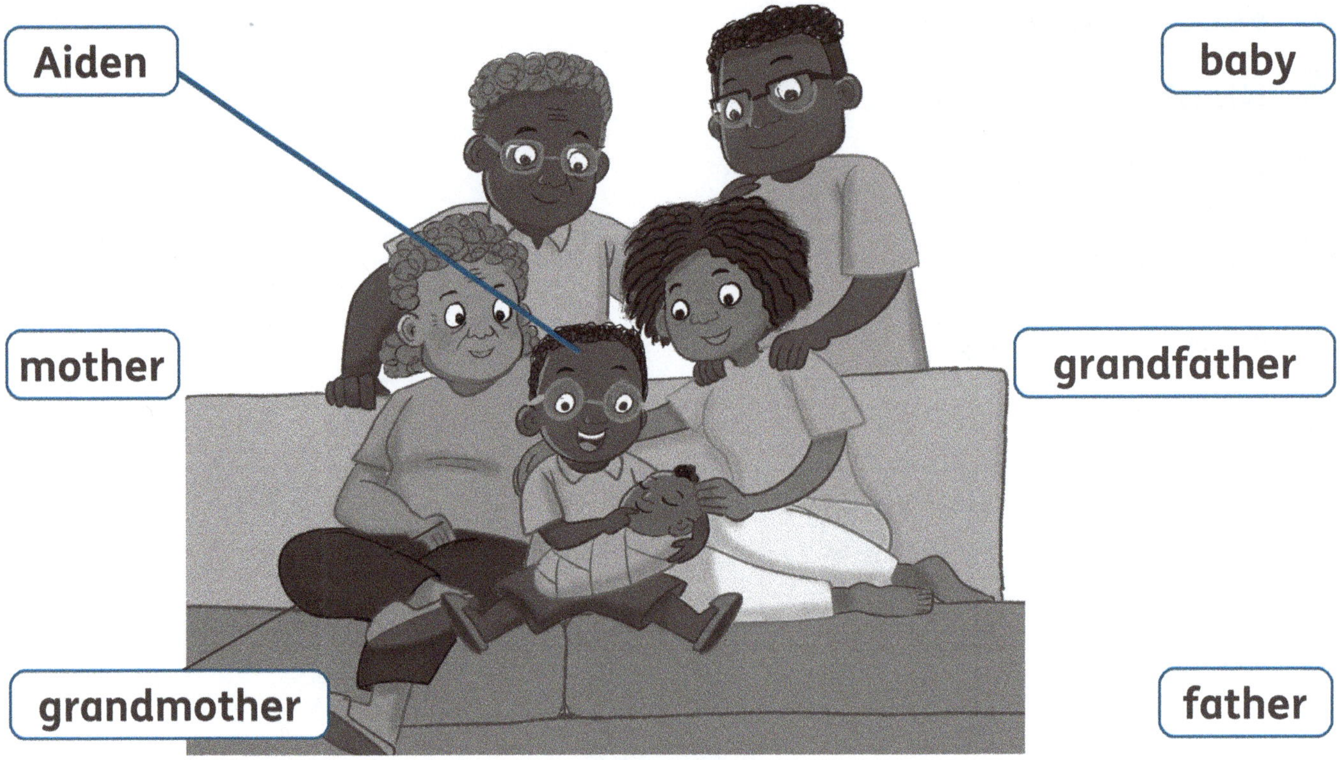

1 Look at the picture of Aiden's family.

Draw a line to match each word with a person in the picture. The first one is done for you.

2 Choose the correct word to complete this sentence. Write the word in the space.

brother **sister**

Aiden has a new baby ______________________.

- Answer questions about a story

Ask someone to read you part of the story of *Aiden and the new baby.*

Grandma arrived first. She rushed in to hug the baby but she forgot to hug Aiden. Grandad came next. He sat and smiled at the baby but he forgot to come outside to explore. Then, in came Uncle Joseph. He spun the baby round and round but he forgot to watch Aiden climbing trees. Last of all came Auntie Mary. She chatted to Mummy but she forgot to read Aiden a story.

1 Who arrived first? Tick the correct answer.

Uncle Joseph ☐

Grandma ☐

Auntie Mary ☐

2 How do you think Aiden felt when all the visitors forgot about him? Circle one word.

happy **cold** **sad**

Talking about the past

Language

We use **simple past** to talk about things that happened before the present time and have finished.

I played football last week.

✔ Ask someone to read the pairs of sentences to you. Tick the sentence that is in the past.

1 Aiden looked at ants yesterday. ☐

Aiden looks at ants. ☐

2 Grandma cooks chicken. ☐

Grandma cooked chicken last night. ☐

3 I play with the baby. ☐

I played with the baby. ☐

Talking about the future

- Say what might happen next
- Talk about the future

1 What do you think Aiden, Grandad and Uncle Joseph will do? Draw a picture.

Language

We use **'will'** to talk about **future** actions and things that have not happened yet.

I **will** visit Grandma tomorrow.

2 Where will you go tomorrow? Think of your own idea to finish this sentence. Write in the space.

Tomorrow I will ____________________________________.

- Answer questions about non-fiction

Baby facts

Ask someone to read these baby facts to you.

Baby facts	
	**A baby who is 6 months old:** • **knows their own name** • **can try some soft food from a spoon** • **learns to sit up** • **learns to roll over.**

Read the questions and circle the correct answer each time. The first one is done for you.

Does a 6-month-old baby know their own name?

yes (circled) **no**

1 Can a baby try soft food when they are 6 months old?

yes **no**

2 What does a 6-month-old baby learn to do?

sit up **play football**

3 How does a 6-month-old baby move around?

walk **crawl** **roll over**

- Use plurals

Plurals

Language

We use **plurals** when we want to talk about more than one of something:

one **brother** → two **brothers**

Sometimes, we use a new word when we are talking about more than one of something:

one **child** → three **children**

Write the correct word to complete each sentence about this picture.

sister **children** **brothers**

1 I have two big ________________.

2 I have one little ________________.

3 There are four ________________ in my family.

How did Femi feel?

Ask someone to read the text to you.

Femi was upset because she lost her teddy. Aiden and Daddy searched and searched. Aiden found the teddy on the washing line. He gave it to Femi and she was happy again.

1 Draw lines from the numbers to the pictures to show the order that these things happened.

1 •

2 •

3 •

2 Draw two pictures to show how Femi's feelings changed during the story.

At the **beginning**, Femi felt:	At the **end**, Femi felt:

Look at the picture. Circle the correct answers.

1 What did Femi lose?

teddy **doll**

2 Who found the thing that was lost?

Daddy **Aiden**

3 Put these words into the correct order to write a caption for the picture above.

found lost Aiden teddy the

Tip Use a capital letter at the beginning of a sentence. Use a full stop at the end.

Writing a story

- Create a story
- Begin to use capital letters and full stops for sentences

Look at the picture. Use these words to write three sentences about Baby Femi and Aiden.

Aiden happy sad

1 Femi was ______________________

2 ______________________ played a game with her.

3 Aiden helped Femi feel ______________________

Check that your sentence:

☐	starts with a capital letter
☐	ends with a full stop
☐	makes sense when you read it out loud.

Unit 1 Reflection

Look back at all the activities in this unit.
How do you feel about what you have done?

1 Colour one face.

2 Look at the checklist. Think about the things you have learned.
Colour the smiley face for the things you feel confident about.

I can answer questions about a story.	
I can talk about the past.	
I can talk about the future.	
I can use words for more than one of something.	
I can write a sentence with a capital letter and a full stop.	

2 All about water

- Read words

Student Book page 16

Words about water

Read the words about water out loud:

tap   wet   rain   waves

Choose one of the words to complete each sentence. Write it in the space. The first one is done for you.

1 Water feels <u>wet</u>.

2 Drops of water from the sky are called ______________________.

3 We can drink water from a ______________________.

4 We can hear crashing ______________________.

- Answer questions about a non-fiction text

Ask someone to read you the water facts.

When water gets very cold, it freezes and changes from liquid into solid. This is called ice. When water gets very hot, it turns from liquid into gas. This is called water vapour.

1 Draw lines to link each label to the correct picture.

liquid ● ● 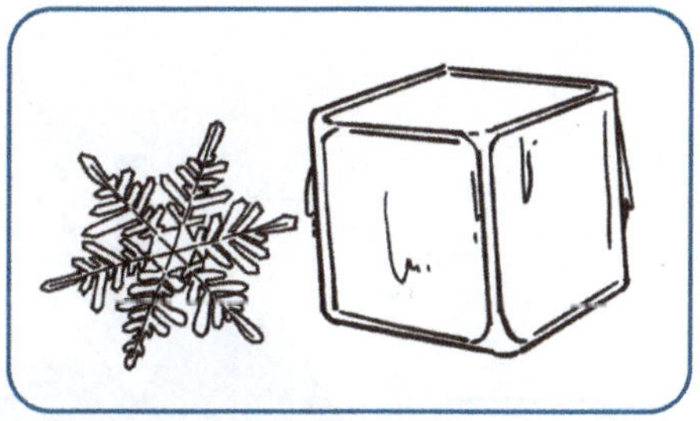

solid ● ● 

gas ● ● 

2 What does water turn into when it freezes?
Circle the correct answer.

vapour   **rock**   **ice**

Student Book page 18

- Answer questions about a non-fiction text
- Use a picture and labels to find facts

The water cycle

Look at the picture and ask someone to read you the information.

The water on our planet is always moving.
This is called the water cycle.

sun

rain

cloud

wind

sea

1 Draw a line to match each label with the correct part of the water cycle picture.

2 Look at the picture to help you answer the questions.

a What heats up the water?
Circle the correct answer.

sun **moon** **stars**

b Where does the rain fall down from?
Circle the correct answer.

clouds **birds** **aeroplanes**

- Answer questions about a non-fiction text
- Use a picture and labels to find facts

Collecting rainwater

Ask someone to read you the information.

The rain falls on the roof and runs down the drainpipe. You attach the pipe to a big barrel. The barrel stores the rainwater until you need it. There is a tap on the barrel. You can use it to fill up a watering can and water your plants.

1 Choose the correct word to fill in the missing label:

box **barrel** **bag**

2 Where does the rainwater go? Draw lines from the numbers to show the correct order. The first one is done for you.

1 •
2 •
3 •
4 •

• Rain goes into the barrel.
• Rain falls on the roof.
• Use rainwater to fill a watering can.
• Rain runs down the pipe.

- Read instructions
- Write a sentence

Instructions

The pictures show you how to wash your hands but they are muddled up.

1

1 Write a number next to each picture to show the correct order. The first one is done for you.

Language

Instructions give us information about how to do something. Each sentence starts with a verb. The numbers tell us what order to do things in.

2 Look at the first picture. Write an instruction to go with the picture. You can use these words to help you.

wet hands

Adding -ing to verbs

Language

When we talk about an action we are doing right now, we add -**ing** to the end of the verb (action word).

read + **ing** = read**ing**   I am read**ing**.

Put these jumbled words in the correct order to make a sentence. The first one is done for you.

1 What is this boy doing?

drinking. is He

He is drinking.

2 What is this girl doing?

is plants. watering She

3 What is this boy doing?

He washing hands. is his

- Answer questions about a story

An important job

Ask someone to read you Latoya's story.

Grandad gave me an important job to do. I had to water the tomato plants every day. I felt very proud.

But I was busy on Saturday, busy on Sunday and busy on Monday. I forgot to do my job. On Tuesday, I saw the plants wilting and drooping. I felt very sad. I gave them lots of water. On Wednesday, the plants looked tall and strong again. I jumped for joy!

1 How did Latoya feel at the beginning of the story? Circle the correct word.

scared **proud** **bored**

2 Why did Latoya feel sad in the middle of the story? Tick the correct answer.

The watering can was too heavy. ☐

The plants were wilting and drooping. ☐

3 Draw a picture to show how Latoya felt at the end of the story:

- Read words
- Write some words

1 Look at the picture and read the labels.

2 Use the words from the labels to finish the sentences:

The plant is ______________________________.

The soil is too ____________________________.

3 What does the plant need? Write a sentence.
Use these words to help you.

needs **water**

____

- Write a sentence
- Give an instruction

Writing a sentence

Ask someone to read you the information.

Children need to drink about five cups of water a day. This helps to keep their bodies healthy and helps their brains work well.

1 What do children need to drink? Tick the correct answer.

five cups of water ☐ two bottles of fizzy drink ☐

2 Write an instruction in a sentence. You can use these words to help you.

water cups drink

____

____

Check that your sentence:

☐	has a capital letter at the beginning	☐	makes sense
☐	has a full stop at the end	☐	has correct spellings.

Unit 2 Reflection

Look back at all the activities in this unit.
How do you feel about what you have done?

1 Colour one face.

2 Look at the checklist. Think about the things you have learned.
Colour the smiley face for the things you feel confident about.

I can answer questions about a non-fiction text.	
I can find out facts using pictures and labels.	
I can write a sentence with a capital letter and full stop.	
I can write a sentence to give an instruction.	

3 Animals

- Read words

Student Book page 29

Animal names

1 Read the animal names.

goat **crab**

2 Choose the correct animal name to complete each sentence. The first one is done for you.

a This is not a crab.

b It is a ______________________________

3 Choose the correct number to complete this sentence:

It has ______ legs.

2 **4** **8**

4 Choose the correct word to complete this sentence:

It eats ______________________________

fish **grass** **sweets**

- Find pairs of rhyming words
- Make a list of rhyming words

Rhyming words

Language

Rhyming words have the same sound at the end. You can hear the rhyme when you say the words out loud. Poems and songs often have rhyming words.

Bird rhymes with **word.**

1 Read the words. Draw lines to match the rhyming pairs.

goat ●	● jab
bat ●	● lake
crab ●	● hat
snake ●	● float

2 Make a list of words that rhyme with **bat**:

hat

______

______

______

______

- Count syllables in words
- Write a two-syllable word

Syllables

Language

A **syllable** is part of a word that you say in one go when you read it out loud. Words can contain one syllable, two syllables or even more.

Shoe has one syllable, **tur/key** has two syllables.

1 Read the animal names. Count the syllables and write 1 or 2 in the box. The first one is done for you.

chicken (chick/en) [2]	frog [ ]	parrot [ ]
cat [ ]	monkey [ ]	dog [ ]

2 Think of another animal with two syllables in its name. Draw a picture and write a name label. You can use one of these pictures to help you.

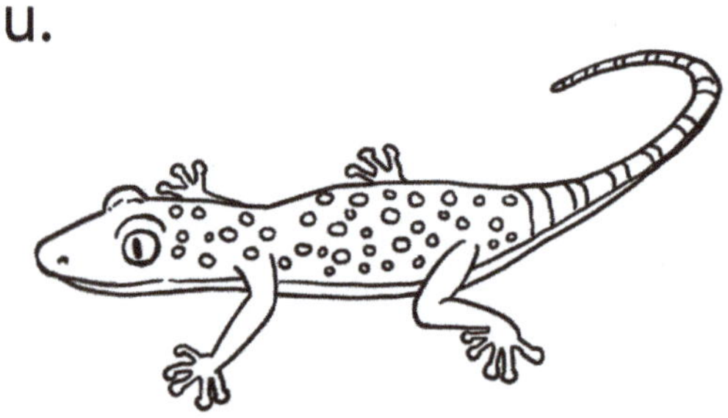

- Respond to rhyme
- Use rhyming words

A counting rhyme

Ask someone to read you the counting rhyme with missing words.

Choose the rhyming word to fill the gap each time. Write it in the space.

1 Parrot one
parrot two,
parrot flapped
and away it ______________________

flew **hopped**

2 Turtle three,
turtle four,
turtle swam,
to the ______________________

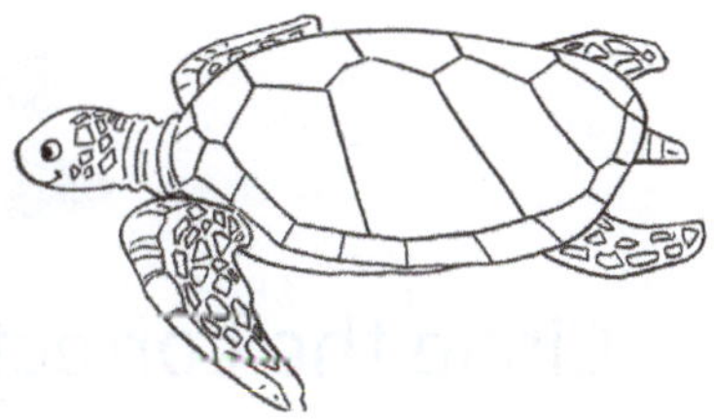

shop **shore**

3 Chicken five,
chicken six,
chicken leading
a line of ______________________

chicks **ducks**

- Make rhyming sentences

Rhyming sentences

Ask someone to read you the silly sentences about animals.

1 Draw lines to match the pairs of rhyming sentences. The first one is done for you.

See the butterfly.	It is riding in a cab.
Look at the goat.	It is up in the sky.
Here is a cat.	It is sitting in a boat.
Can you see the crab?	It is wearing a hat.

2 Look at the picture.

Circle the correct word to answer each question.

a What animal can you see?

snake **cow**

b What is it eating?

sweets **cake**

3 Make up your own rhyming sentences about the picture by filling in the missing words:

a Look at the ______________________

b It is eating the ______________________

- Write a sentence
- Use phonetic knowledge to help write words

1 What is your favourite animal? Draw a picture of it.

2 Write a caption for the picture by finishing these sentences. You can use these words to help you.

big **furry** **funny** **fast** **cute** **fierce** **small**

This is a ______________________

I like it because ____

____

- Sort letters that make different sounds

Letters that make different sounds

Language

Some letters can be pronounced in different ways.

Crab starts with a hard **c**.
Centipede starts with a soft **c** like the **/s/** in 'snake'.

Goat starts with a hard **g**.
Giraffe starts with a soft **g** like the **/j/** in 'jam'.

1 Ask someone to read these words beginning with '**c**' to you:

cent car cow cereal circle cup

2 Write each word in the correct column.

Hard 'c' like crab	Soft 'c' like centipede

3 Look at the pictures and say the word. Draw a circle around the word that begins with a soft **g**.

giant

gorilla

- Describe an animal
- Use phonemes to help write words with one syllable or two syllables

1 Look at the picture of the chicken. What does it look like? What does it do? What sound does it make? What does it eat?

2 Write the words and phrases that you think of. The first one is done for you.

feathers

chicken

Writing a poem

- Write a poem
- Use phonic knowledge to help write words with one syllable or two syllables
- Use the layout for a poem

Use the chicken words and phrases to help you write a poem about a chicken. Your poem does not have to rhyme.

1 Copy the word 'chicken' at the beginning of each line. Then write a word or phrase to describe the chicken.

2 Say each line out loud before you write it.

3 Segment the phonemes to help you spell the words.

Line 1: Chicken + what it looks like

____

Line 2: Chicken + the sound it makes

____

Line 3: Chicken + what it does

____

Line 4: Chicken, chicken

____

Unit 3 Reflection

Look back at all the activities in this unit.
How do you feel about what you have done?

1 Colour one face.

2 Look at the checklist. Think about the things you have learned.
Colour the smiley face for the things you feel confident about.

I can make a list of words that rhyme.	
I can count the syllables in words.	
I know that the letters 'c' and 'g' can be pronounced in different ways.	
I can write words to describe an animal.	
I can make up a poem about an animal.	

4 People who help us

- Read words

Student Book page 40

Who are these people?

1 Read the names of people who help us. Match each name to something they use to do their job. The first one is done for you.

dentist
firefighter
doctor
police

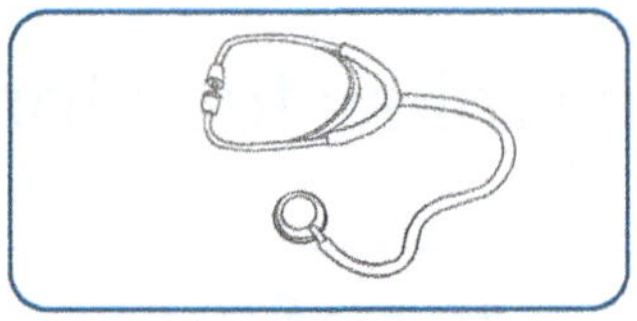

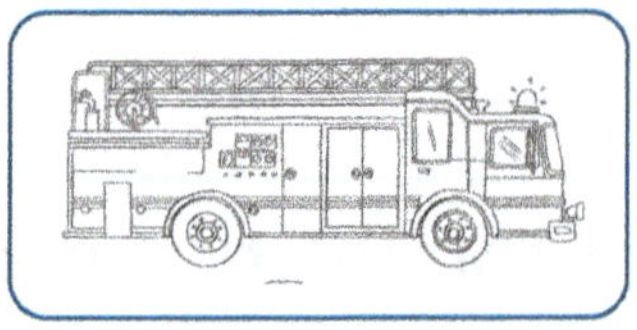

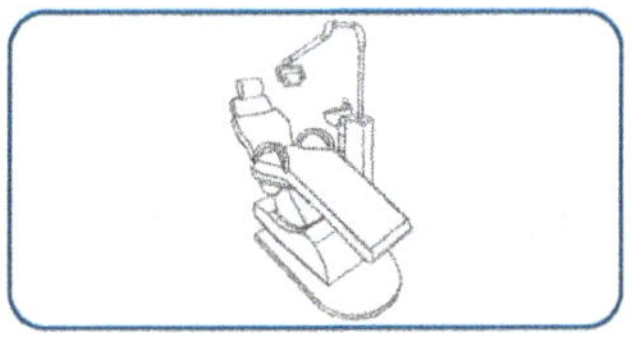

2 Read the sentences about this person who helps us. Choose the correct word to complete each sentence.

hospital sick nurse

a I am a ________________

b I work in a ________________

c I help people who are ________________

- Answer questions about a story

Understanding a story

Ask someone to read you the first part of the story *Priya at the fire station.*

Priya was on a school trip to the fire station. All the children were excited. They couldn't wait to see the big, red fire truck. Priya was the most excited of all. Her dad was a firefighter and he would be there to meet them.

The children arrived at the fire station. Priya's dad talked about his job. "I am **proud** to be a firefighter," he said. "I help to save lives when I put out fires."

Priya gave a big smile. She felt so proud of her brave dad.

"Now it is time to show you around the fire station. Follow me!" said Priya's dad.

Glossary

proud feeling pleased about something you have done or something someone close to you has done

1 Where did Priya's class go on their school trip? Circle the correct answer.

to the shops **to the fire station** **to the park**

2 Who showed the class around? Circle the correct answer.

Priya's dad **Latoya's grandad** **Omar's mum**

3 What does Priya's dad do as part of his job? Tick **two** correct answers.

He saves lives. ☐ He cooks food. ☐

He sails boats. ☐ He puts out fires. ☐

- Write labels
- Read some words
- Write a sentence

Writing labels

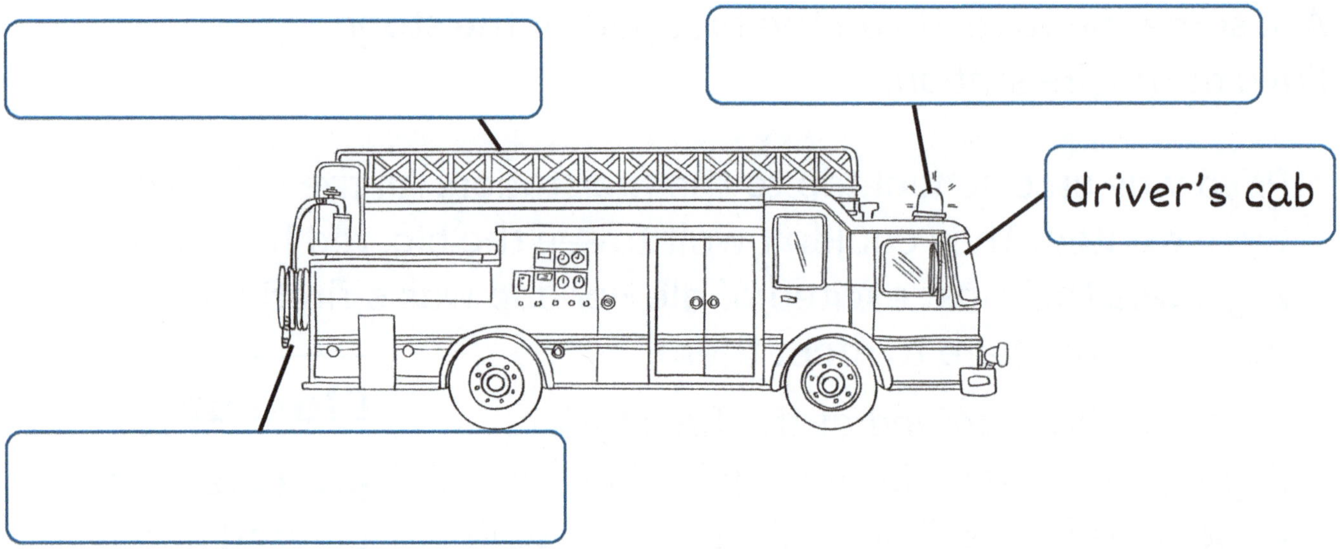

1 Look at the picture of the fire truck. Choose the correct words to write labels for different parts of the fire truck. The first one is done for you.

driver's cab **long hose** **tall ladder** **blue light**

2 What is each part of the fire truck for? Draw lines to match the information to the correct label. The first one is done for you.

blue lights	to reach up high
hose	to warn cars that it is coming
ladder	to spray water

3 What colour is a fire truck? Put these words into the correct order to write your answer. Remember to put a capital letter and a full stop in the correct places.

is **red** **it**

- Use new words
- Read some words
- Say what might happen next

Thinking about a story

Ask someone to read you part of the story *Priya at the fire station.*

Priya's dad gathered all the children together. He explained that the bell was ringing because there was an **emergency**. The firefighters rushed to put on their special clothes. Then, they collected their equipment and jumped into the fire truck. Priya's dad got into the driver's seat. He called out of the window, "There is a fire! We must go and help!"

1 What does the word **emergency** mean? Ask someone to read the answers. Tick the correct ones. The first one is done for you.

when someone is in danger	✔
when someone needs help straight away	
when someone is safe and well	

2 What did Priya's dad call out of the window? Choose the correct word to complete each sentence in the speech bubble.

There is a __________!

help **fire**

We must go and __________!

3 Read the sentences. Choose one sentence and draw a picture to show what the firefighters will do next. Copy the sentence below your picture. Use extra paper.

They will put out a fire.

They will get a cat down from a tree.

- Begin to use simple prefixes
- Read some words

Words with the same root

Language

We can use some words like building blocks. We can add sets of letters to the **root** word to make a new word with a different meaning.

happy → un + happy = unhappy

1 Draw a face that is happy and a face that is unhappy.

happy **unhappy**

2 Make new words by adding **un-** to the beginning of each word. The first one is done for you.

un + kind = unkind   un + pack = ________

un + tidy = ________   un + well = ________

3 Ask someone to read you these sentences. Choose the correct **un-** word to complete each one. The first one is done for you.

a My brother will not play with me. He is being unkind.

b I have come back from my holiday. I have a suitcase to ________.

c Look at all this mess! This room is ________.

d I am feeling ill. I am ________.

- Understand a text
- Answer questions about a text
- Write a sentence

Answering questions

Ask someone to read you the information about a person who helps us.

I am a doctor and I help people who are ill. The people who come to see me are called my patients. They tell me how they are feeling and I find out what is wrong with them. I use my stethoscope to listen to their heart beating and check their breathing. I look into their ears, eyes and throats. I decide what treatment they need to get better.

1 Who does the doctor help? Put the words in the correct order to make a sentence.

helps **who** **she** **ill** **people** **are**

____

2 What are the people who go to see the doctor called? Circle the correct answer.

patients **pupils** **pilots**

3 What does the doctor use her stethoscope for? Ask someone to read the sentences. Tick the correct answer.

To listen to the patient's heart. ☐

To look into the patient's ears. ☐

To talk about how the patient is feeling. ☐

- Use pronouns
- Write a sentence

Using pronouns

Language

We use the pronoun **I** when we are talking about ourselves. We use the pronouns **he, she** or **they** when we are talking about someone else.

I am a firefighter. **He/She** is a firefighter. **They** are firefighters.

firefighter

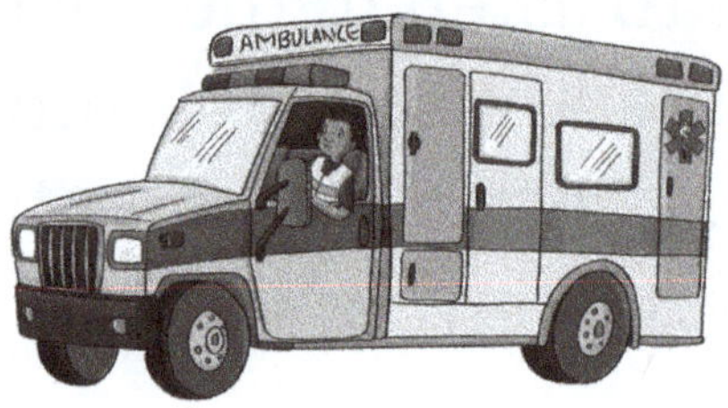

ambulance driver

dentist

police officers

1 Look at the pictures. Choose the correct pronoun to complete each sentence. Say it out loud. The first one is done for you.

a ____They____ are firefighters.

b ______________ is an ambulance driver.

c ______________ is a dentist.

d ______________ are police officers.

she he they

2 Put the words in the correct order to complete the speech bubble for the ambulance driver.

is ambulance my this

I am an ambulance driver.

____

- Identify the beginning, middle and end of a story
- Write a story using pictures and captions

Telling a story

1 Look at the pictures and read the sentences. Match each sentence to the correct picture to tell the story.

1 The firefighters came.

2 They got the cat down.

3 The cat got stuck in the tree.

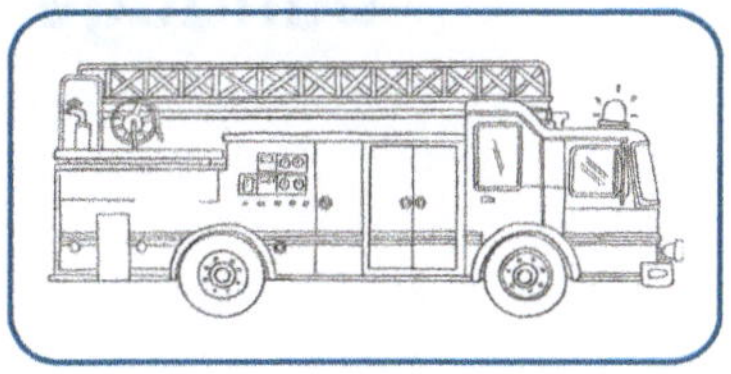

2 What do you think happened after the firefighter brought the cat down from the tree? Draw a picture of your idea.

3 Write a sentence to go with your picture. You can use this sentence starter or think of your own idea.

The cat was ______________________________.

- Make up a story with a beginning, middle and end
- Write a story using pictures and captions

Writing a story

1 Read the beginning of the story. Choose the correct word to complete the sentence:

an ambulance **a fire truck** **a police car**

Priya fell over at the park. Mum called ______________________

2 Look at the picture. Write a sentence about what the ambulance driver did to help Priya. You can use these words to help you.

bandage **arm**

____

3 Ask someone to read the sentences about what happened at the end. Tick the one you want to use for your story.

Priya went to hospital in the ambulance. ☐

Priya's arm felt much better, so Mum took her home. ☐

4 Draw a picture to show what happened at the end of the story. Use extra paper.

Unit 4 Reflection

Look back at all the activities in this unit.
How do you feel about what you have done?

1 Colour one face.

2 Look at the checklist. Think about the things you have learned.
Colour the smiley face for the things you feel confident about.

I can write a sentence with a capital letter and full stop.	
I can answer questions about a story I have listened to.	
I can read some words with un- at the beginning.	
I can use a pronoun in a sentence.	
I can make up a story using pictures and captions.	

5 Night-time creatures

- Spell some words
- Read some words
- Write a sentence

Student Book page 53

Animals active at night

1 Say the names of the creatures that are active at night. Finish writing the label for each one.

b ____________

o ____________

m ____________

r ____________

2 What does the sky look like at night? Complete these sentences. You can use these words to help you.

dark moon black stars

At night, the sky looks ____________________

You can see ____________________

Nocturnal creatures

- Answer questions about a text
- Use new words

Ask someone to read you the non-fiction text.

Did you know that when you go to bed, lots of creatures are just waking up? Animals, insects and birds that are active at night time are called nocturnal. Many of these creatures can see in the dark. Others have excellent hearing and a strong sense of smell. They can find their way and hunt for **prey** even when there is no light.

Glossary

prey an animal that is hunted by another animal for food

1 What does **nocturnal** mean? Circle the correct answer.

asleep during the night **awake and active during the night**

active during the night and the day

2 How do these creatures find their way at night? Put these words into the correct order to make a sentence. Write your sentence.

can dark the see they in

____

3 Owls hunt for insects, mice and frogs. Look at the pictures. Colour the ones that are the owl's **prey**.

- Read some words
- Answer questions about a text

Answering questions

1 Look at the picture. Read the caption and the label.

Bats do not have feathers on their wings.

2 Do bats have wings? Circle your answer: **yes** **no**

3 Do bats have feathers? Circle your answer: **yes** **no**

4 Put these words into the correct order to make another sentence about bats. Write your sentence.

sleep daytime bats the in

____

Sounds at night

Ask someone to read you the non-fiction text.

If you go outside at night time, you might hear all sorts of sounds.

- Some owls make a screeching sound while they are flying.
- Crickets make a chirping sound by rubbing their wings together.
- Tiny frogs in the trees make a whistling sound.
- Bats make sounds that are too high for human ears to hear.

1 What sounds do these night-time creatures make? Draw lines to match each creature with the correct sound.

whistle ● ● 

screech ● ● 

chirp ● ● 

2 What part of their body do crickets use to make a sound? Circle the correct answer.

mouth **legs** **wings**

3 Can human ears hear the sounds that bats make? Circle your answer.

yes **no**

- Find out about letters that make different sounds
- Read some words
- Spell some words

Letters that make different sounds

Language

When the letter **y** is at the end of a word, it can be pronounced in different ways.

The letter **y** makes an **/ee/** sound in **happy**.
The letter **y** makes an **/ie/** sound in **sky**.

1 Ask someone to read these words ending with **-y** to you.

mummy try fly story funny my

2 Write each word in the correct column.

/ee/ like happy	/ie/ like sky

3 Read the unfinished sentence below, then choose the best word to complete it. Write the word and read the whole sentence again.

The hungry bats fly in the dark ______________________

shy try sky fry

4 Look at the picture and say what you can see. Write the correct word to complete the caption.

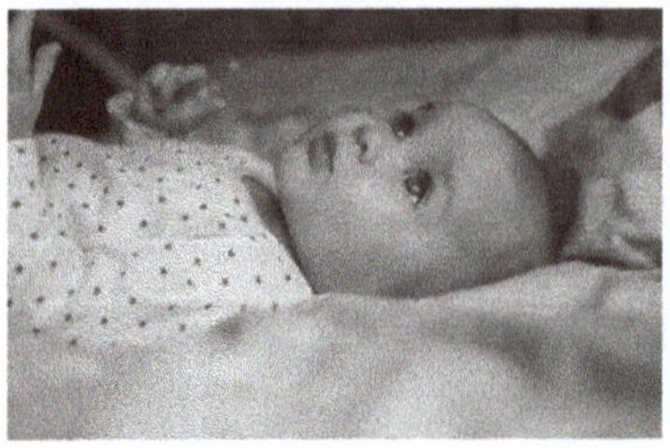

This is a ______________________

- Make up sentences with two ideas using 'and'
- Write a sentence

Making and writing sentences

bat

owl

ocelot

1 Look at the pictures and ask someone to read the sentence parts below to you. Draw lines to match two parts of a sentence about each creature. The first one is done for you.

These animals hunt at night ●	● and then they pounce.
Owls have feathers ●	● and some eat fruit.
Many bats eat insects ●	● and sleep during the day.
Ocelots track their prey ●	● and they fly silently.

2 Choose the correct words to complete the sentence about night-time creatures.

like eat and

Fruit bats ____________ to eat figs ____________

owls like to ____________ mice.

3 Make up a sentence about ocelots. Join two ideas using 'and'. You can use these words to help you.

hunt at night have sharp claws have spots and stripes

Ocelots ________________________________

and ________________________________

Using apostrophes

- Begin to learn how to use an apostrophe
- Read some words

Language

We use **an apostrophe and the letter 's'** after a naming word as a quick way to show that **something belongs to somebody**.

the owl's wings means **the wings that belong to the owl**

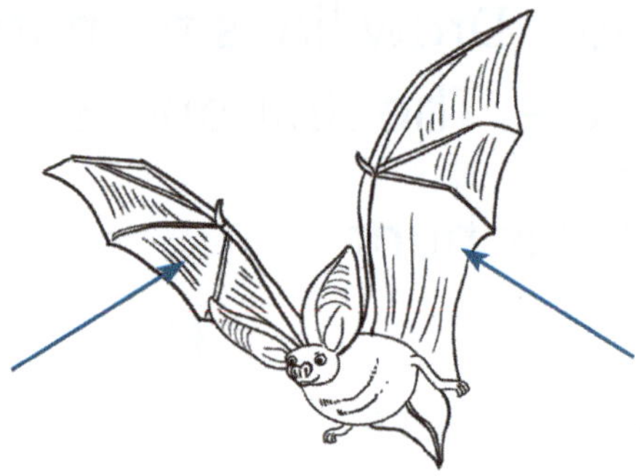

________________________ ________________________

1 Look at the pictures. Write the labels in the correct places.

the bat's wings **Omar's goggles**

2 Ask someone to read the sentences to you. Tick the correct answer.

The goggles belong to Omar. ☐

The goggles belong to his brother. ☐

The goggles belong to his friend. ☐

3 Who do the wings belong to? Complete the sentence.

The wings belong to ________________________

Using words that tell us where something is

- Use words that tell us where something is
- Read some words
- Write a sentence

Language

We can use words such as **above, next to** or **below** to say **where something is**. These words answer the question 'Where is it?'

Omar is **next to** the tree.

1 Look at the picture. Where is the owl? Tick the correct answer.

next to the tree ☐

above the tree ☐

below the tree ☐

2 Where is the frog? Complete the sentence. You can use these words to help you.

next to **below** **tree** **cricket**

The frog is ______________________________

3 Draw a picture of yourself. Draw the moon **above** you. Draw the grass **below** you. Draw a night-time creature **next to** you. Use a separate piece of paper.

- Begin to write a non-fiction text
- Use headings and labels

Writing non-fiction

Ask someone to read you the information about whistling frogs.

These tiny frogs are no more than three centimetres long. They hide in damp, dark places during the day. They are active at night when they climb up into trees and bushes. They have suckers on their toes to help them climb. The males make a whistling sound. They hunt for spiders and ants to eat.

1 What is the name of this night-time creature? Write a heading.

____

2 What do they have on their toes to help them climb? Circle the correct answer. Copy the word to make a label for the picture.

suckers **claws** **shoes**

← ______________________

3 What do they eat? Write a sentence.

This night-time creature eats ______________________

Unit 5 Reflection

Look back at all the activities in this unit.
How do you feel about what you have done?

1 Colour one face.

2 Look at the checklist. Think about the things you have learned.
Colour the smiley face for the things you feel confident about.

I can read words with the same letter but a different sound.	
I can use 'and' to join two ideas in a sentence.	
I can use the words 'above', 'below' and 'next to' to say where something is.	
I understand that an apostrophe can show that a thing belongs to someone.	
I can write a heading, label and a fact for a non-fiction text.	

6 Favourite food

- Read some words
- Use new words

Student Book pages 66–67

What do you like to eat?

1 Look at the pictures of food. Read the labels. Draw lines to match each picture to the correct label.

chicken • • 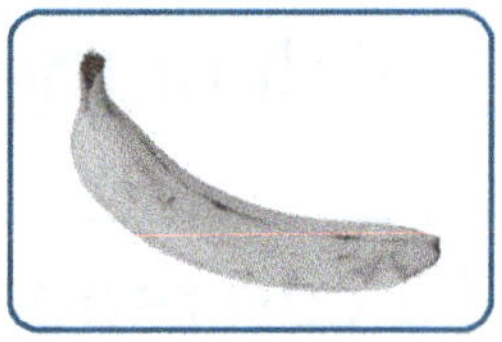

mango • • 

banana • • 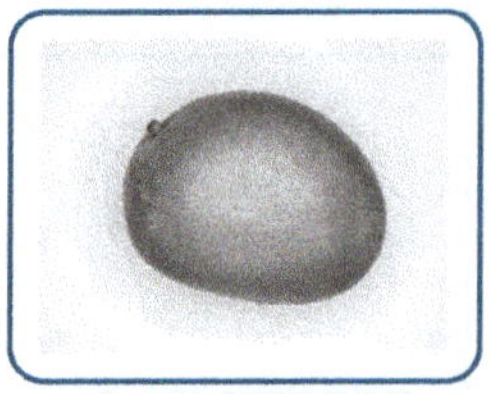

rice • • 

2 Choose a type of food from the pictures. Write a sentence to say why you like it. You can use these words to help you.

it is hot **it is crunchy** **it is tasty** **it is sweet**

I like ______________________ because ______________________

____

- Respond to a poem
- Read some words
- Make a list of rhyming words

Rice and peas

Ask someone to read you a part of the poem 'Rice and peas'.

Chorus:
Rice and peas
Peas and rice
Red peas, green peas
Always nice!
Rachael Sutherland

1 Read the words for the chorus. The lines are in the wrong order. Draw lines to match the numbers to the correct line from the poem to show which one is first, second, third and fourth.

1 •	• Red peas, green peas
2 •	• Peas and rice
3 •	• Always nice!
4 •	• Rice and peas

2 Read the words. Circle the words that rhyme with 'rice'.

nice	**rich**	**cake**	**spice**
dice	**like**	**mice**	**kite**

3 Write more words that rhyme with 'rice'.

rice, ice, twice, ______________, ______________, ______________

- Find rhyming words
- Write rhyming sentences

Latoya's new verse

Ask someone to read you Latoya's new verse for the poem.

Chicken and fries
So good to munch,
I like chicken
For my ____________

1 Choose the best word to finish Latoya's poem.
Circle the word that rhymes with 'munch'.

snack **supper** **lunch** **dinner**

2 Read the words. Draw lines to match the pairs of rhyming words.
The first one is done for you.

cherry	boat
fish	boot
goat	berry
fruit	dish

3 Read the sentences. Add a word to make the sentences rhyme.

Do you like crispy fish?
It is my favourite ______________________________ .

- Read some words
- Write a sentence

Describing

1 Look at the picture of the pineapple. Draw lines to match the labels with the correct part of the picture.

skin

leaves

flesh

2 Think about what a pineapple is like on the outside and the inside. Read the sentence starters and match each one with the correct sentence ending. The first one is done for you.

I can touch ...	... bright, yellow flesh.
I can see ...	... hard, spiky leaves.
I can touch ...	... rough, thick skin.

3 What does pineapple taste like? Put these words into the correct order to make a sentence.

sweet tastes pineapple juicy and

____

- Learn how to spell more plurals
- Spell some words

Plurals for words ending in 'o' and 'y'

Language

When we want to talk about **more than one of something**, we often **add an 's'** to the end of the word. Sometimes we need to change the last few letters of the word.

Words ending in **-o** ⟶ add **-es**
Words ending in **y** ⟶ take off the **y**, and add **-ies**

one **mango** ⟶ two **mangoes**   one **cherry** ⟶ two **cherries**

1 Ask someone to help you read these words.
Circle the ones that are plurals.

jelly **tomatoes** **jellies** **mango** **mangoes** **tomato**

2 Write the plurals for these words. The first one is done for you.

one berry ⟶ two berries

one patty ⟶ two ______

one potato ⟶ two ______

3 Read the sentence. Look at the pictures and choose the correct word to fill each gap.

eggs

tomatoes

I went to the shop and I got six ______ and three ______.

- Answer questions about a poem
- Find rhyming words

Answering questions about a poem

Ask someone to read you this poem about making food.

I've got sugar, flour and eggs,
What shall I make?

I think I'll add some milk
To make fluffy pancakes.

First whisk everything together,
Then fry them in the pan,

Flip them over,
And then eat as fast as you can!

Rachael Sutherland

1 What is this poem about? Put these words into the correct order to make a sentence.

making is about pancakes it

____

2 What ingredients get used to make the pancakes?
Circle the correct answers.

mango flour eggs pepper milk bread sugar

3 Write more words on this list of words that rhyme with 'pan'.

pan, can, plan, ____________, ____________, ____________

- Learn how to use words for things you can't count
- Read some words

Uncountable nouns

Language

Some **nouns** can be **counted**. We can show whether there is one of something by putting **'a'** or **'an'** in front of a word. We can show if there is more than one by putting **a number** in front of the word and making it into a plural.

an **egg** ⟶ two **eggs**

Some **nouns cannot be counted**. We cannot put 'a', 'an' or a number in front of these words.

milk

1 Which of these naming words are uncountable? Write each word under the correct heading. The first one is done for you.

~~milk~~ **mango** **meat** **pancake** **bread**

Countable	Uncountable
	milk

2 Read the sentences. Choose the correct word to complete each sentence.

a **some**

a I have cooked __________________ meat.

b Would you like __________________ bread?

c Here is __________________ pancake for you to eat.

- Read some words
- Use new words

Action words

Ask someone to read you this rhyme about eating.

I like to nibble, bite and chew,
I gobble, crunch and munch.
My mouth is working very hard,
When I eat my lunch!

Rachael Sutherland

1 Read the action words in the word cloud. All the action words are to do with eating. Which six action words are used in the rhyme about eating? Write them on the lines below.

bite **chew** **crunch** **munch** **gobble**
gulp **nibble** **eating** **sip** **lick**

__________ __________ __________

__________ __________ __________

2 What do these action words mean? Draw lines to match each word to the correct definition. The first one is done for you.

munch	eat food quickly
gobble	take small bites
nibble	chew food loudly

3 Imagine you are eating these fries. Write a sentence with an action word to describe what you like to do.

When I eat fries I like to ____________________

- Spell some words
- Write clearly
- Use the correct layout for a poem

Planning and writing a poem

1 What are your favourite drinks?
Ask someone to read you the different sorts of drinks below.
Circle the drinks that you like.

water **milk** **chocolate milk**

soft drinks **fruit juice** **coconut water**

tea **fruit smoothie** **chocolate tea**

2 What are your three favourite drinks? Make a list.
Put them in order with the best thing of all at the end.

1 ______________________________

2 ______________________________

3 ______________________________

3 Write a simple poem about what you like to drink. Use the ideas from your list. Read your poem out loud when you have completed it.

My favourite things to drink

I like to drink ____________________

I love to drink ____________________

But my best drink of all is ____________________

Unit 6 Reflection

Look back at all the activities in this unit.
How do you feel about what you have done?

1 Colour one face.

2 Look at the checklist. Think about the things you have learned.

Colour the smiley face for the things you feel confident about.

I can find pairs of words that rhyme.	
I can continue a string of rhyming words.	
I can spell plurals correctly.	
I can read and write action words for eating.	
I can write a simple poem.	

7 Once upon a time

- Respond to stories
- Write a sentence

Student Book page 78

Understanding traditional stories

1 Look at the pictures of things from different stories. Ask someone to read you the story titles. Draw lines to match each picture to the correct title. The first one is done for you.

Cinderella

Goldilocks and the Three Bears

The Three Billy Goats Gruff

Jack and the Beanstalk

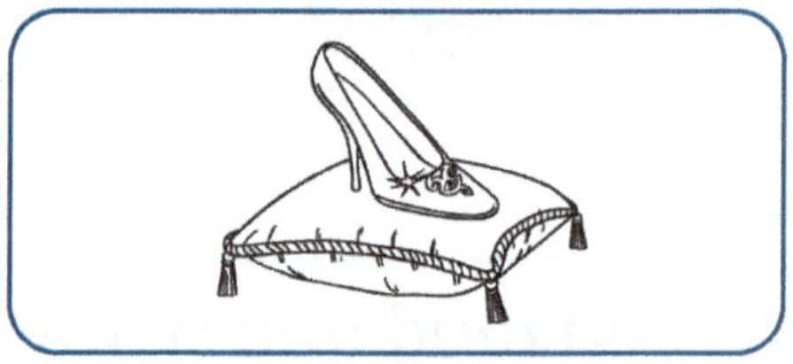

2 How do traditional stories often begin? Put the words into the correct order. Write them in the space to complete the first sentence of a story.

a once time upon

_______________________________ there were three bears.

- Read some words
- Talk about characters
- Write a sentence

Reading a story

Ask someone to read the first part of *The Three Billy Goats Gruff* to you.

Once upon a time, there were three Billy Goats Gruff: Little Billy Goat Gruff, Middle-sized Billy Goat Gruff and Great Big Billy Goat Gruff.

They wanted to go over the bridge to eat the sweet, green grass on the other side. However, a fierce, hungry Troll lived under the bridge. The Troll wanted to gobble them all up.

1 Look at the picture and read the labels. Draw lines to match each label to the correct part of the picture.

Troll

bridge

goats

2 Who is the baddie in this story? Circle one answer.

Little Billy Goat Gruff **the Troll** **Great Big Billy Goat Gruff**

3 Why do the goats want to go over the bridge? Put these words into the correct order. Write a sentence in a speech bubble for them.

to We the want grass. sweet eat

____

____

- Use an increasing range of language
- Read some words

Words that make a sound

Language

Some words **sound like the sound that they are describing.**

buzz – the sound of a bee

splash – the sound of something falling into water

1 Read the words. Circle three words that sound like sounds.

car **splash** **house** **pop** **tick-tock**

2 What sounds do these creatures make? Draw lines to match each picture to the correct sound word.

quack ●　　　● 

buzz ●　　　● 

hiss ●　　　● 

- Read some words
- Learn about apostrophes for missing letters

Using apostrophes

Language

We use an **apostrophe** to show that two words have been squashed together to make a new word. We put the apostrophe in the place where a letter or letters have been missed out to make the new word.

I am is changed to **I'm**

1 Which words have been squashed together to make these new words with apostrophes? Match each one to the correct words.

I'm ●	● He is
It's ●	● Who is
Who's ●	● I am
He's ●	● It is

2 Read the sentence. Circle the words with apostrophes.

It's raining so I'm going home.

3 Read the speech bubble. Rewrite the sentence using a word with an apostrophe.

____

____

- Answer questions about a story
- Respond to a story
- Read some words

Answering questions about a story

Ask someone to read the last part of *The Three Billy Goats Gruff* to you.

Last of all, Great Big Billy Goat Gruff went over the bridge. *TRIP, TRAP, TRIP, TRAP*.

"Who's that trip-trapping over my bridge?" called the Troll.

"It's me, Great Big Billy Goat Gruff," thundered Great Big Billy Goat Gruff.

"I'm going to eat you up!" yelled the Troll.

"Oh no you're not!" replied Great Big Billy Goat Gruff. He put down his head with its enormous horns and ran towards the Troll. He butted that Troll right off the bridge and down, down into the river. Splash! The Troll was never seen again.

Great Big Billy Goat Gruff went to join his brothers. *TRIP, TRAP, TRIP, TRAP*.

The Three Billy Goats Gruff lived happily ever after.

1 How did Great Big Billy Goat Gruff get past the Troll? Circle the correct answer.

He tricked the Troll. **He knocked the Troll down.**

He ran past the Troll.

2 Did the Troll come back to the bridge at the end of the story? Circle the correct answer.

yes **no**

- Talk about characters
- Read some words
- Write a question

Questions

Language

You can use a **question word** at the beginning of a question.

Who What Where Why When How

You can turn a sentence into a question by putting words in a different order and adding a question mark at the end.

You have got sharp teeth. → **Have you got sharp teeth?**

1 Match each question to the correct character's speech bubble.

Who are you?

What do you like to eat?

How did you knock the Troll down?

I like to eat goats.

I used my horns.

I am Little Billy Goat Gruff.

2 Put these words into the correct order to make a question for the Three Billy Goats Gruff. Remember what to put at the beginning and the end of your question.

you where ? do live

____

3 Read the sentence about the Three Billy Goats Gruff. Circle the correct answer.

They live in a big town. **true** **false**

- Answer questions about a story
- Respond to a story
- Talk about the beginning, middle and end of a story

Understanding different parts of a story

Ask someone to read you a new version of a story that you have heard before.

I was lost in the woods and I was very hungry. I saw a house with the door wide open. Then I saw bowls of delicious porridge and I couldn't help eating it all. I didn't mean to break the chair but the leg fell off when I sat on it. I found a lovely bed to sleep in. I was so surprised to see the bears when I woke up. I ran all the way back home again.

1 Who is telling this story? Tick the correct picture.

 ☐

 ☐

 ☐

2 What did Goldilocks do at the beginning, in the middle and at the end of the story? Draw lines to match each sentence with the correct label.

Beginning ●	● Goldilocks ran home.
Middle ●	● Goldilocks ate the porridge and broke the chair.
End ●	● Goldilocks got lost in the woods.

3 Did Goldilocks mean to break the chair? Circle the correct answer.

Yes, she did mean to break the chair.

No, she didn't mean to break the chair.

- Learn about apostrophes for missing letters
- Read some words

Using apostrophes

Language

We can use words with **apostrophes** to help us ask and answer questions.

would not → **wouldn't** did not → **didn't** could not → **couldn't**

Would you like to eat porridge? No, I **wouldn't**.

1 Which words have been squashed together to make these new words with apostrophes? Match each one to the correct words.

couldn't ●	● do not
didn't ●	● could not
don't ●	● did not

2 Ask someone to read the sentences about The Three Bears. Find the words with apostrophes and draw a circle round each one.

They couldn't eat the porridge because it was too hot.

They didn't see Goldilocks go into the house.

3 Did Baby Bear find Goldilocks asleep in his bed?

Tick the correct answer.

Yes, he did. ☐

No, he didn't. ☐

- Write a story with pictures and captions
- Spell some words
- Write sentences

Writing a story

1 Make up a story about the Troll from *The Three Billy Goats Gruff*. Where did he go? What did he do? What happened in the end? Use these words to give you some ideas.

forest **swamp** **ate crabs**
ate berries **lived happily ever after**

2 Draw three pictures.

3 Write a sentence under each picture to tell your story.

Beginning

____

____

Middle

____

____

End

____

____

Unit 7 Reflection

Look back at all the activities in this unit.
How do you feel about what you have done?

1 Colour one face.

2 Look at the checklist. Think about the things you have learned. Colour the smiley face for the things you feel confident about.

I can predict what might happen in a story.	
I can read words that sound like sounds.	
I can read words with apostrophes.	
I can write a question.	
I can write a story.	

8 Keeping healthy

- Read some words
- Write a sentence

Student Book page 90

Reading and writing

1 Look at the pictures of different things that you can use for exercise. Draw lines to match each one to the correct word. The first one is done for you.

swimming

cycling

football

cricket

2 Which one of these types of exercise would you like to do? Choose the words to complete the sentence.

go swimming **play football** **ride my bike**

I would like to ______________________________

- Read some words
- Answer questions about a text

Reading and answering questions

1 Look at the picture and read the caption at the bottom.

banana

fish

milk

carrot

This plate shows how much of each type of food we should try to eat.

2 Read the labels. Draw lines to match each label with the correct food or drink in the picture.

3 Look at the plate. What sort of food should we eat lots of? Tick **two** correct answers.

fruit ☐ cakes ☐ vegetables ☐

4 Why do we need to eat food that is good for us? Put the words into the correct order to complete the sentence.

bodies keep healthy our

We need to eat good food to ______________________________

____

- Read some words
- Answer questions about a text

Reading non-fiction text

Ask someone to read the information about staying fit to you.

Exercise is an important part of staying healthy. Exercise can include running in the playground, dancing, swimming, playing football or any other physical activity that you enjoy.

- Exercising our bodies keeps our muscles and bones strong.
- Exercise gives us energy.
- Exercise keeps our minds sharp.

If you can play outdoors, that is even better. Fresh air and sunshine are good for you too!

1 What different types of exercise are there?
Read the words and circle three types of exercise.

running **swimming** **sleeping** **dancing** **eating**

2 What keeps our muscles and bones strong?
Read the words and circle the correct answer.

doing exercise **sitting still** **washing hands**

3 Read the sentence and decide whether it is true or false.
Circle the correct answer.

Fresh air and sunshine help to keep us healthy.

true **false**

How to brush your teeth

1 Read the instructions for brushing your teeth. Ask someone to help you if you get stuck.

1. Put toothpaste on your toothbrush.
2. Brush your front teeth.
3. Brush your back teeth.
4. Spit out the toothpaste.

2 Look at the jumbled pictures. Write a number next to each picture to show the correct order.

 ☐

 ☐

 ☐

 ☐

3 What do you do at the end? Tick the correct answer.

Swallow the toothpaste. ☐

Spit out the toothpaste. ☐

• Read and spell plurals

Understanding words that mean more than one thing

Language

When we want to talk about **more than one thing**, we usually add **-s**.

one bed → two **beds**

Sometimes, we need to change the word. The plural has a different spelling.

one foot → two **feet**

1 Read the two lists of words. Draw lines to match the pairs of words. The first one is done for you.

One thing	**More than one thing**
child	teeth
tooth	men
foot	children
hand	feet
man	hands

2 Read the sentence. Circle the word that is a plural.

Children need a good long sleep every night.

3 Choose the correct word to complete this sentence.

foot feet teeth tooth

I brush my ______________________ twice a day.

- Read some words
- Write a sentence

Reading and writing sentences

1 Read the tips for staying healthy.
Write the correct word in each space.

food **need** **sleep**

Tips for staying healthy

We need to eat good ____________________.

We need to drink lots of water.

We ____________________ to keep fit.

We need to keep clean.

We need lots of ____________________.

2 Look at the picture. Which tip is this child good at doing? Choose the correct words to complete the speech bubble.

sleeping **drinking water** **keeping clean**

I am good at

____

____________________.

- Answer questions about a story
- Write a sentence

Maya does gymnastics

Ask someone to read the beginning of the story about Maya to you.

On Saturdays, Maya goes to gymnastics club. It is her favourite time of the week.

First, Maya does her warm-up exercises. She stretches slowly, bends gracefully and then jumps quickly.

Next, she practises turning cartwheels until she can do them perfectly. Maya's arms are strong.

Then, she climbs up onto the beam and walks carefully along it. Maya is very brave. "Well done, Maya. You balanced beautifully," says the coach.

1 What sort of exercise does Maya do at her club?
Circle the correct answer.

swimming **gymnastics** **netball**

2 What does she do to warm up? Tick three correct answers.

stretches ☐ hops ☐ bends ☐ jumps ☐

3 Look at the picture. What is Maya doing?
Put the words in the correct order to write a sentence.

on Maya the beam. balance is

____

____

Student Book page 97

- Use an increasing range of language
- Begin to use simple suffixes
- Read some words

Understanding adverbs

Language

Adverbs tell us how something is done.
We often use an adverb after a verb.

How did she run? **quickly, slowly**

Adverbs are often made by adding **-ly** to a describing word (adjective).

quick + **ly** = **quickly**

Some adverbs don't have **-ly** at the end.

fast **well**

1 Read the sentences and look at the pictures. Draw lines to match each sentence with the correct picture.

I can shout loudly. ●   ● 

I can tiptoe quietly. ●   ● 

I can run fast. ●   ● 

2 Find the adverbs in the sentences above. Circle each adverb.

3 Choose the correct adverb to complete this sentence.

loudly **happily** **carefully**

Remember to cross the road ______________________.

- Write a non-fiction text
- Write in sentences with full stops
- Spell some words
- Join two ideas in a sentence using 'and'

Writing instructions

Ask someone to read the information about doing the bear crawl.

This is how you do the bear crawl. You put your hands on the floor. You put your feet on the floor. You move your hands and your feet. You see how fast you can go.

1 Put these words together to join two ideas in a sentence. Write out the sentence.

and your feet **on the floor.** **Put your hands**

____

____

2 Complete a set of instructions about how to do the bear crawl.

How to do the ______________________________

First, ______________________________ and

______________________________.

Next, ______________________________ and

______________________________.

Try to go ______________________________.

Unit 8 Reflection

Look back at all the activities in this unit.
How do you feel about what you have done?

1 Colour one face.

2 Look at the checklist. Think about the things you have learned.
Colour the smiley face for the things you feel confident about.

I can answer questions about a text I have read.	
I can use 'and' to join two ideas in a sentence.	
I can read and spell some words for more than one of something.	
I can read some adverbs ending in -ly.	
I can write instructions for an exercise.	

9 Weather

- Read some words
- Write a sentence

Student Book page 102

Matching words with pictures

1 Look at the pictures of the different weather symbols. Draw lines to match each picture to the correct label. The first one is done for you.

sunny snowy stormy rainy cloudy

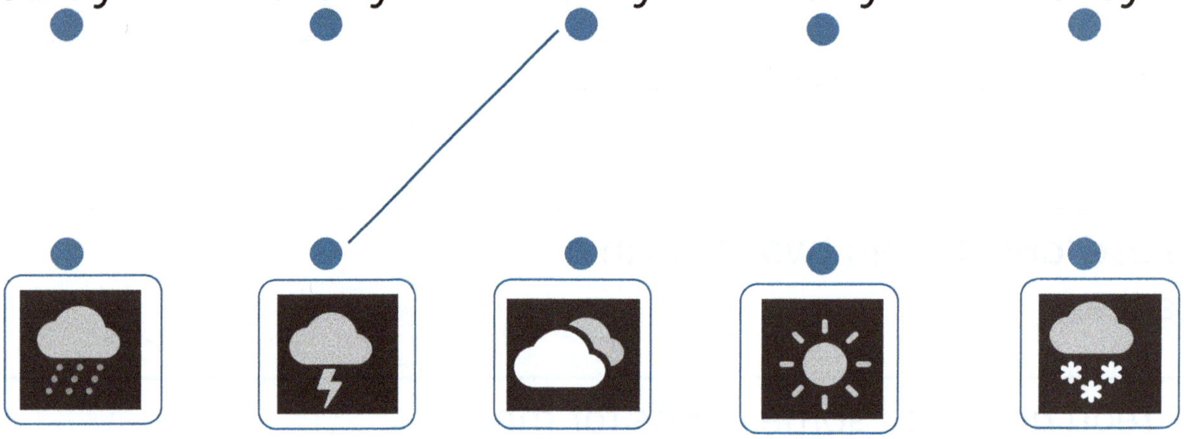

2 Read this sentence. Draw a picture showing the correct type of weather on a separate piece of paper.

It is a rainy day.

3 What type of weather do you like? Fill in the gaps to complete this sentence. You can use some of these words to help you.

sunny rainy stormy cloudy
hot cool exciting fun

I like ______________________________ weather

because it is ______________________________.

- Find rhyming words
- Read some words
- Write some words

Watch the weather

Ask someone to read the poem 'Watch the weather' to you.

Watch the weather changing
All day long,
See a rainbow in the sky,
And then it's gone.

[Chorus]

Sun and clouds,
Showers of rain,
Strong winds blow,
Then sun again.

Listen to the weather,
Fierce winds howl,
Thunder bangs and crashes,
Rain hammers down.

Rachael Sutherland

1 Read the chorus again. Fill in the missing words.

Sun and clouds,

Showers of ____________

Strong winds blow,

Then sun ______________

2 Read the words. Circle the words that rhyme with 'rain'.

chain **farm** **pain** **read** **lane**

3 Write more words on this list of words that rhyme with 'rain'.

rain, again, main, ________________, ________________,

________________, ________________

- Read some words
- Use different tenses

Hot and cold

Ask someone to read the 'Hot and cold' poem to you.

The weather is cold today.
It is as cold as an ice cream,
Colder than a freezing shower,
Colder than the coldest
iceberg.

The weather was hot yesterday.
It was as hot as a chili-pepper,
Hotter than a barbeque,
Hotter than the hottest volcano.

Rachael Sutherland

Language

The **verb** in a sentence shows when something happens.

The weather **is** hot today. The weather **was** hot yesterday.
The weather **will be** hot tomorrow.

1 Read the sentence and circle the correct answer.

The poem says that the weather is hot today.

true **false**

2 Draw lines to match each sentence with when it happened.

It will be cold tomorrow. ●	● happened in the past
It was hot yesterday. ●	● happening now
It is rainy today. ●	● will happen in the future

3 Put these words into the correct order to make a sentence about the weather in the future. Remember to start with a capital letter and end with a full stop.

tomorrow will it rain

___

- Understand and use similes
- Read some words
- Write some words

Using similes

Language

A **simile** is when you compare two different things using 'like' or 'as'. Similes help us to imagine things.

freezing cold **like** an iceberg

as hot **as** a volcano

1 Find the missing words to complete each of the similes. Choose one of the words from the word cloud and write it in the correct space. The first one is done for you.

sun **ice** **~~lightning~~** **thunder**

as fast as lightning

as cold as ______

as loud as ______

as bright as the ______

2 Look at the picture. What do the raindrops look like? Circle the simile you like best.

a like tears from the clouds

b like sparkling diamonds

c like a grey curtain

3 What does the rain sound like? Make up a simile. You can choose one of these ideas or think of your own.

a hammer banging **a band marching** **a tap dripping**

The rain sounds like ______.

- Answer questions about a poem
- Read some words
- Use alliteration

Weather forecast

Ask someone to read the poem 'Weather forecast' to you.

Here is the weather forecast for tomorrow:
In the morning
the sun will sparkle and sizzle.
In the afternoon
the wind will whistle and whirl.
In the evening
the rain will rush down like rivers.

Rachael Sutherland

1 The poem says that there will be three different types of weather tomorrow. What are they?
Tick three correct answers.

rainy ☐ snowy ☐ windy ☐ sunny ☐

2 Read the words. Draw lines to match the pairs of words that begin with the same letter. The first one is done for you.

rushing	wind
sparkling	rain
whirling	sun

3 Choose the words beginning with 's' to write a sentence about the sun.

crash scorch sparkle rise sizzle whistle smile

The sun will ______________________, ______________________,

______________________ and ______________________.

- Answer questions about a poem
- Read some words

Rain

Ask someone to read the poem 'Rain' to you.

First one drop and then another,
Rain is falling down.
The shower gets stronger, pitter patter,
Puddles on the ground.
Now heavy rain like stamping boots,
Hammers all around.

Rachael Sutherland

1 Read the sentences about what happens in the poem.
Use these words in the correct place to complete each sentence.

heavy **one** **stronger**

First, there was ______________________ drop of rain.

Then, the rain got ______________________.

At the end, the rain was very ______________________.

2 What sound does the rain make in the poem?
Circle the correct answer.

spit spot **pitter patter** **drip drip**

3 What is the heavy rain compared to? Circle the correct answer.

stamping boots **sticks and stones** **beating drums**

- Read some words
- Write a sentence

Reading and writing sentences

1 Look at the pictures. Which one shows dry weather and which one shows wet weather? Write the correct label below each picture.

wet weather | dry weather

2 Read the words describing the two pictures.
Circle the words that describe the **wet weather**.

dark sky **bright sun** **gentle breeze** **heavy rain**

blue sky **feeling hot** **loud thunder** **feeling cold**

3 What sort of weather makes you feel happy? Draw a picture and complete the sentence.

I feel happy when the weather is ________________.

- Read some words
- Use new words
- Write some words

Using quantifiers in sentences

clouds

raindrops

puddle

1 Look at the picture. Draw lines to match each label to the correct part of the picture.

Language

We use words called **quantifiers** when we are answering questions like 'How much ...?', 'How many ...?', 'Was there any ...?'

lots of **not a lot of** **lots** **none** **no**

We put the quantifier before the noun in a sentence.

There are **lots of** clouds in the sky.

2 How many people can you see in the picture?
Circle the correct answer.

lots **none** **one**

3 Read the sentences about the picture. Choose the correct word to complete each one.

lots of **no**

There is ________________ snow in the picture.

There are ________________ raindrops in the picture.

Planning and writing a poem

- Spell some words
- Write clearly
- Use the correct layout for a poem

1 How would you describe the sun and sky in this picture? Read the words and decide whether they are describing the sun or the sky. Make a list under the correct heading.

bright blue **round** **clear** **shining**
scorching **yellow** **hot** **as blue as the ocean**

sun	sky
____________________	____________________
____________________	____________________
____________________	____________________

2 What could you compare the clouds to? Choose your favourite words to complete this sentence.

fluffy sheep **soft pillows** **cotton candy**

The clouds are like ______________________________.

3 Write a simple poem about a sunny day. Choose describing words and phrases from your lists. Finish with a line about how it makes you feel. Read your poem out loud when you have completed it.

The sun is ______________________________.

The sky is ______________________________.

The clouds are like ______________________________.

I feel ______________________________.

Unit 9 Reflection

Look back at all the activities in this unit.
How do you feel about what you have done?

1 Colour one face.

2 Look at the checklist. Think about the things you have learned.
Colour the smiley face for the things you feel confident about.

I can find pairs of rhyming words.	
I can write a string of rhyming words.	
I can use different tenses to talk about the past or the future.	
I can make up a simile.	
I can write a poem about the weather.	

Unit	Topic	Texts	Reading
1	Families	**Fiction:** *Aiden and the new baby* (RS) **Non-fiction:** Baby facts (RS)	2R1, 2R2, 2R4, 2R5, 2R6
2	All about water	**Non-fiction:** Water facts (RS) **Fiction:** *An important job* (RS)	1R2, 2R1, 2R2 2R5, 2R6, 2R9, 2R11
3	Animals	**Poetry: Rhythm and rhyme** A counting rhyme (RS)	1R11, 2R1, 2R6, 2R7, 2R9, 2R10, 2R11, 2R12, 2R14, 2R15
4	People who help us	**Fiction:** *Priya at the fire station* (RS) **Non-fiction:** I am a doctor ...	2R1, 2R4, 2R5, 2R6 2R9, 2R11, 2R13
5	Night-time creatures	**Non-fiction:** Facts about nocturnal creatures (RS)	2R1, 2R2, 2R6 2R9, 2R11, 2R12, 2R13
6	Favourite food	**Poetry:** Poems about food (RS)	2R1, 2R6, 2R7, 2R9, 2R11, 2R13, 2R14
7	Once upon a time	**Fiction:** *The Three Billy Goats Gruff* (extracts; retold by RS)	2R1, 2R4, 2R5, 2R6, 2R7 2R9, 2R11, 2R12, 2R13, 2R15
8	Keeping healthy	**Non-fiction:** Staying fit *(SH)* **Fiction:** *Maya does gymnastics* (RS)	2R1, 2R2, 2R6, 2R9, 2R11, 2R12, 2R13, 2R15
9	Weather	**Poetry:** Weather poems (RS)	2R1, 2R6, 2R7, 2R9, 2R11, 2R13, 2R14, 2R15

Notes: Original texts written by Rachael Sutherland (RS) and Suzette Hussey (SH).

Writing	Language structure and vocabulary
2W1, 2W5 **2W7, 2W10, 2W12** Write a simple story. Write a caption.	**2L1, 2L2, 2L6** Plurals. Reviewing past tense. Simple future tense.
2W1, 2W3, 2W6 **2W8, 2W9, 2W10, 2W11, 2W12** Write a sentence.	**2L2, 2L3, 2L6** Suffix -ing for present continuous.
2W2, 2W3, 2W6, 2W11 Write a simple poem.	**2L2, 2L7** Subordinating conjunction 'because' in a sentence: Letters that make different sounds.
2W2, 2W3, 2W5, 2W6, 2W7 **2W9, 2W10** **2W11, 2W12** Write a story with a beginning, middle and end.	**2L2, 2L3, 2L4** Root words Possessive pronouns and adjectives. Sentence punctuation.
2W1, 2W2, 2W3, 2W6, **2W7, 2W9, 2W10, 2W11, 2W12** Write a non-fiction text with a heading, label and a fact.	**2L2, 2L5, 2L7** Using connective 'and' in a sentence. Prepositions of position. Apostrophe for possession with names.
2W2, 2W3, 2W9, **2W10, 2W11, 2W12** Write a simple poem.	**2L1, 2L2** Plurals that change ending e.g. words ending in 'y' and 'o'. Countable/uncountable nouns.
2W3, 2W5, 2W7, **2W9, 2W11, 2W12** Write own version of a traditional story.	**2L4, 2L7** Apostrophe for common contractions, e.g. who's, don't, can't. Question forms e.g. Would you ... ?
2W1, 2W3, 2W6 **2W9, 2W10, 2W11, 2W12** Write a set of simple instructions.	**2L1, 2L3, 2L4, 2L5** Plurals that change form e.g. tooth/teeth, foot/feet. Adverbs ending -ly e.g. slowly, quickly etc.
2W3, 2W6 **2W9, 2W11, 2W12** Write a poem.	**2L1, 2L2, 2L5, 2L6** Introducing similes and alliteration. Reviewing past, present and future tense. Quantifiers: lots, a lot of, not a lot, none.